SUPERSTARS OF POKER
TEXAS HOLD'EM

Greg
"Fossilman"
Raymer

SUPERSTARS OF POKER
TEXAS HOLD'EM

Doyle "Texas Dolly" Brunson

Johnny "Oriental Express" Chan

Antonio "The Magician" Esfandiari

Chris "Jesus" Ferguson

Gus "The Great Dane" Hansen

Jennifer Harman

Phil "The Poker Brat" Hellmuth

Phil "Tiger Woods of Poker" Ivey

Phil "Unabomber" Laak

Howard "The Professor" Lederer

Chris Moneymaker

Daniel "Kid Poker" Negreanu

Greg "Fossilman" Raymer

Texas Hold'em: The Learning Curve of Life

SUPERSTARS OF POKER
TEXAS HOLD'EM

Greg "Fossilman" Raymer

Mitch Roycroft

Mason Crest Publishers

Greg "Fossilman" Raymer

Produced by 21st Century Publishing and Communications, Inc.
Editorial by Harding House Publishing Services, Inc.

MASON CREST PUBLISHERS INC.
370 Reed Road
Broomall, Pennsylvania 19008
(866) MCP-BOOK (toll free)
www.masoncrest.com

Printed in the United States.

First Printing

9 8 7 6 5 4 3 2 1

Library of Congress Cataloging-in-Publication Data

Roycroft, Mitch.
    Greg "Fossilman" Raymer / by Mitch Roycroft.
      p. cm. — (Superstars of poker)
    Includes bibliographical references and index.
    Hardback edition: ISBN-13: 978-1-4222-0228-9
    Paperback edition: ISBN-13: 978-1-4222-0380-4
  1. Raymer, Greg. 2. Poker players—Biography. 3. Poker. I. Title.
GV1250.2.R3R69 2008
795.412092—dc22
[B]   2007024799

Publisher's notes:
All quotations in this book come from original sources, and contain the spelling and grammatical inconsistencies of the original text.

The Web sites mentioned in this book were active at the time of publication. The publisher is not responsible for Web sites that have changed their addresses or discontinued operation since the date of publication. The publisher will review and update the Web site addresses each time the book is reprinted.

CONTENTS

INTRODUCTION

by the North American Poker Council

FOR GOOD OR ILL, TEENS LOVE POKER. IT'S BECOME the Friday-night activity of choice for many adolescents. Some adults are pleased, some definitely aren't. So what's the reality?

Well, here are some facts:

- Poker keeps teens occupied in someone's living room or kitchen, rather than out drinking and cruising.

- Poker teaches young adults to pick up on social cues. As they learn to understand "tells," they're gaining insights that help them in a variety of situations.

- Poker develops the portions of the brain that deal with mathematical skills. In today's world where math and the sciences are important to many career paths, those skills are vital.

- Poker helps young adults learn self-control. Kids who have tantrums when things don't go their way don't last long in poker games. Learning to wear a "poker face" helps teens control their up-and-down emotions so they can excel in academic, social, and professional situations.

- Poker gives kids a better understanding of their own mental states. You can't learn self-control without realizing what it is you're controlling. Poker helps adolescents recognize their feelings, which in turn, allows them to get a handle on their emotions.

So if all that's true, why are so many parents and school officials concerned about the new rush of poker-playing teens? In large part, it's because of the moral baggage poker carries; while poker has a long history as a North American pastime, it has an equally long reputation for being shady and sinful. Only recently has poker begun to shake off this reputation and enter the mainstream.

Unfortunately, however, there's good reason for concern when it comes to teens and poker. Here's why: teens who play poker face a real risk of gambling addiction.

So should parents and educators shout a loud, resounding "NO!" when it comes to young adults and poker? Well, that seldom works when it comes to teens; poker is out there, and it's being heavily marketed to the younger generation. A far better choice is to take a look at the realities and assist young adults in developing the skills they'll need to handle poker's challenges wisely.

That's what this series does. It allows teens to learn from the best: the superstars who win time after time. These stars have important life lessons to offer teenagers, and their message is clear: you're not going to have the mental capacity to win if you drink, use drugs, don't get enough sleep, don't eat healthy, or if you allow poker to consume your life.

And isn't that a great message for teens and adults alike to hear?

The Fossilman

♠ ♠ ♠ ♠

IN 2004, A MAN NAMED GREG RAYMER TURNED A $160 "investment" into a $5 million payday. He wasn't a businessman, banker, or famous actor. He didn't make his millions in real estate, the stock market, movies, or even the lottery. He was a lawyer-turned-poker player, and he won the money playing a game.

Payday

Greg had been an **amateur** poker player for years. In 2004, he entered an online tournament at PokerStars.com. The event was a **satellite** tournament for the World Series of Poker—the WSOP, the largest and most

Who would have thought it was possible? Greg Raymer for one. He spent $160 to enter an online poker tournament, and turned it into $10,000—and a seat at the World Series of Poker main event. But that wasn't all for the Fossilman; he took home the event's $5 million-dollar prize.

prestigious poker tournament on earth. It cost $160 to enter the online satellite event. Whoever won would receive the $10,000 buy-in fee to the World Series' main event.

Greg won that online satellite tournament and the chance to compete against the toughest poker competition alive. A few months later, he was playing in the WSOP main event. There were 2,576 people playing, making it the largest live (rather than online) poker game in history to that date. Some of the players were amateurs taking their once-in-a-lifetime shot at the big prize. Some were former world champions hoping to reclaim the title. Many were hardened pros with decades of experience grinding away in cash and tournament games.

Greg was just another nameless face in a sea of hopefuls. But through days of grinding play, the sea parted, like it did when Moses led the Children of Israel away from their captors—and player after player fell beneath the flood of other players' victories. In the end, only ten were left standing. They sat down at the final table, and after five solid hours of intense play, Greg was the last player left. In an article for Blind Bet Poker.com, author Greg Cavouras summed up the action at the final table:

> **❝Greg Raymer came into this tournament as an extremely distant longshot; he took on the best players in the business, and had the cards to back him up. The result was a confident solid player who held the chip lead at the final table from start to finish and was rewarded with a $5 million dollar payday, the largest in Poker history!❞**

The Fossilman

Greg's big win at the WSOP was the end of his day job. He gave up working as a lawyer and began playing poker full time. Like most pros, he soon came to be known on the **circuit** by a nickname; in the poker world, Greg is called "Fossilman." On his Web site, www.fossilman.com, Greg describes how he earned his poker moniker:

> **❝In about 1996, my wife took me to a rock and mineral show in San Diego, where we lived at that**

time. I bought an orthoceras fossil because I thought it was neat and would make a great card protector. Many of the other players at the Oceanside Card Club also thought it was neat. I then had the idea to go back to the show, buy more fossils, and sell them at a profit. And it worked quite well. So, I went into the business of selling fossils whenever I played poker, as a way of more quickly building my bankroll so I could get into bigger games.**"**

In addition to bringing rocks to the table, Greg is also famous on the poker circuit for his eyewear. Whenever he's at a major tournament,

With his win at the 2004 World Series of Poker No Limit Texas Hold'em main event, Greg had to make a career decision—continue as a patent lawyer, or turn his multimillion-dollar win into a career in professional poker. He didn't take long to decide, opting to play poker full time. He wasn't happy as an attorney anyway.

Greg dons a pair of opaque sunglasses with **holographic** lizard eyes on the lenses. On his Web site, Greg describes how the sunglasses evolved from being a joke to becoming part of his standard poker gear:

> **"I bought my lizard-eye 3-D hologram sunglasses ... on a family vacation prior to my first WSOP main event in 2002. I thought it would be a funny joke to**

Greg's little sideline of selling fossils and rocks earned him the nickname "Fossilman." But that's not the only distinctive thing about the poker champ. Most players wear sunglasses at the table, but Greg's are special—holographic lizard-eye lenses. For some reason, those glasses can cause some opponents to get flustered—and lose.

put them on in the middle of an important hand. However, when I first did so, instead of making everybody laugh, the glasses freaked out my opponent in the hand, and caused him to fold. Since then, I've found that some of my opponents are very uncomfortable playing against me because of the glasses, and therefore I've continued to wear them during major tournaments. **"**

A Unique Player

Greg's success in unnerving his opponents with his unusual glasses spawned many imitators. In an interview with James Hardy for HoldEm-Back.com, Greg joked that copying him probably wasn't a good idea:

"I looked like a dork, but a unique dork, when I first did it. They probably look like a copycat dork to most of the world."

Greg's joke says a lot about his personality. He's known for being humble, down to earth, and—despite being a world champion—never taking himself too seriously. An article on PokerStars.com describes his character as quite the opposite of what one would expect of a world champion:

"Meeting [Greg] for the first time is quite a bewildering experience. The first thought that comes to mind is—*where's the swagger*? Of all the champions crowned king of the poker world . . . [Greg] is, without a doubt, the least pretentious of them all."

Greg's personality might be kind and relaxed, but his poker style is aggressive and merciless. Some new players assume Greg, because of his gentle demeanor, will be a pushover in tough games. They are usually surprised then to see the Fossilman sweep their chips away. In the game of poker, deception is everywhere. Don't be fooled by appearances. Greg "Fossilman" Raymer is a master of the game.

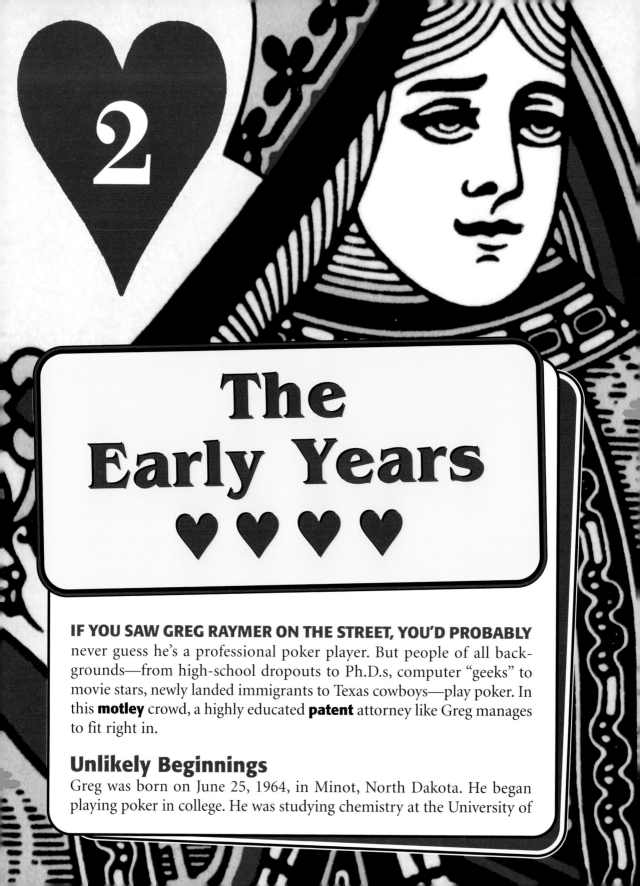

The Early Years

♥ ♥ ♥ ♥

IF YOU SAW GREG RAYMER ON THE STREET, YOU'D PROBABLY never guess he's a professional poker player. But people of all backgrounds—from high-school dropouts to Ph.D.s, computer "geeks" to movie stars, newly landed immigrants to Texas cowboys—play poker. In this **motley** crowd, a highly educated **patent** attorney like Greg manages to fit right in.

Unlikely Beginnings

Greg was born on June 25, 1964, in Minot, North Dakota. He began playing poker in college. He was studying chemistry at the University of

Greg Raymer began playing poker while studying chemistry at the University of Missouri. After graduation from college, he moved on to graduate school—and casinos, clubs, and blackjack. His ability to count cards came in handy, earning him money to pay for grad school. Though he practiced law, Greg's biggest success came when he practiced his undeclared major—poker.

Missouri, and poker was a fun way to pass a Saturday night with friends. Those college poker games were nothing serious; they usually played for nickels and dimes.

After earning his bachelor's degree, Greg studied for his master's degree at the University of Minnesota. He also started going to casinos, where he played blackjack, a game that combines strategy and luck. Like all casino games, the odds in blackjack are with the house. But some exceptional players can count the cards as they fall around the table, calculate the odds, and beat the game. Greg was one of these people, and counting cards helped pay for his master's degree in biochemistry.

Greg went on to study law at the University of Minnesota. He graduated in 1992 and began working at a large law firm in Chicago. As he explains on his Web site, that's where he began playing "real" poker:

"While looking for a blackjack game, I found a poker game, and played for fun. I had already learned the basics of the game while in college playing in nickel-dime-quarter games in my fraternity and with my friends in grad school and law school. However, in those little games we were all pretty pathetic, and none of us knew how to play very well. Once I started playing 3-6 limit poker in Chicago, I decided I should learn to play well, and bought myself some poker books to study."

The Rat Race

Poker was a pleasant pastime for Greg—something to enjoy when he wasn't at work. Unfortunately, that wasn't very often. It didn't take him long to realize that the rat race—a sixty- to eighty-hour work week in a pressure-cooker atmosphere—wasn't his idea of an enjoyable life.

Poker, meanwhile, was extremely enjoyable for Greg, but his wife worried. After all, plenty of people get sucked into poker and other forms of gambling, becoming addicted to the action, convinced that they will win—but going broke from their delusions. On his Web site, Greg describes the deal he and his wife made:

"In about 1995 I made a deal with my wife that I would have a bankroll for poker, separate from my income, savings, and investments. This bankroll was $1000. If I played and won, I could do whatever I wanted with the money, e.g., move up in limits, buy stuff, whatever. However, if I lost all of the money, I had promised to quit playing poker forever."

Despite a sixty- to eighty-hour workweek, Greg found time to play poker. He wasn't happy, though, as a member of the rat race; he wanted to play poker full time. He and his wife Cheryl talked about it and came up with a plan. If he lost his poker bankroll, he'd quit playing once and for all.

Building a Bankroll

The deal Greg made with his wife was a wise one, and most successful poker players live by similar rules. They keep their bankroll separate from all other wealth. When they win, they replenish or build their bankroll, and then invest anything that's left over in savings, real estate,

Greg is a smart poker player. He has a bankroll that finances his poker playing. Winnings go back into the bankroll and into savings plans. Losses are taken from the bankroll, not from investments or other income. This way, players—and their families—know they have something left to support them should they go broke.

retirement funds—anything that keeps the money safe from gambling. When they lose, they make the money back at the poker table rather than dip into their investments to replenish the bankroll.

The poker players who don't keep their bankroll separate from their larger wealth operate in a dangerous world where compulsive gambling and poor money management can cause total financial ruin. In an occupation where hundreds, thousands, and occasionally even millions of dollars can change hands in a single game, intelligent money management is the only way to survive.

Greg was not only surviving, but succeeding. Instead of losing that original $1000, he built upon it and steadily moved up to bigger games. His day job, however, wasn't bringing him the same sense of satisfaction. For about six years, Greg did his time as a patent attorney with large firms, first in Chicago and then in San Diego. After that, he'd had enough.

In 1998, Greg got a new job with pharmaceutical giant Pfizer, Inc. He relocated to Connecticut in 1999 and began playing poker at the Foxwoods Resort and Casino. He didn't know it at the time, but he wouldn't have to work that day job for many more years. Playing poker was going to change his life.

Evolution and Revolution

♣ ♣ ♣ ♣

AT THE TURN OF THE CENTURY, AS GREG RAYMER STOOD
poised to make a giant leap into the professional poker world, poker was
about to make a huge leap of its own. Over the years, poker had evolved
from a backroom game to a popular pastime, and now it was about to
become a television phenomenon.

Today poker is the third-most-watched sport on television. Millions
of people play the game at home, online, and in casinos. Even those who

It did not take long for Greg Raymer to become a popular player on the professional poker circuit. Though players were not crazy about the glasses, the lenses were a hit with the fans, setting him apart from the other players. He came on the scene at the right time—poker was on its way to becoming a worldwide phenomenon.

don't play poker are touched by the game. Having "an ace up one's sleeve," putting on your "poker face," "upping the ante," and being a "high roller" are just a few of the poker-inspired phrases commonly used in conversation today.

People have played games resembling poker for hundreds of years. Although the exact origins of the game are unclear, versions of poker were being played in America at least as early as the late 1820s. But it wasn't long before the game became associated with crime, violence, and immorality. It's been a long journey from the game's backroom beginnings to its television presence in living rooms around the world today.

The "Dark Ages"

Throughout the twentieth century there was a tension between a public disapproval of games, like poker, that involve gambling, and a private enjoyment of such pastimes. Many Americans, often influenced by religious beliefs, considered gambling immoral and sinful, and poker fell into that category. However, despite common anti-gambling laws, poker was commonly played in people's homes and in clubs.

For most of the century, however, playing poker for a living was definitely not considered a respectable thing to do. People who played poker "professionally" were called "rounders." They traveled from town to town looking for action, avoiding the police who would arrest them, the cheats who would swindle them, and the hijackers who would rob them. They lived in an underground world, and with thousands of dollars changing hands in secret, illegal games, violence often erupted.

Doyle "Texas Dolly" Brunson, a legendary poker player who still competes with the best in the world, began his career as a rounder. In his book, *Super System*, he recalls poker's darker age, describing what Exchange Street—a popular location for poker games in Fort Worth, Texas—was like in those days:

> **"I'd be surprised if you could find a tougher street in the whole world. There were shootings, muggings, robberies, and just about every kind of violence imaginable. The stuff we see on TV today is tame compared to what Exchange Street was like almost any hour of the day."**

PRINT/ONLINE DIGITAL

MAGAZINE

♠AMERICAN Poker Player

APPMagazine.com   July/August 2006 $4.95

COVER STORY

High Stakes Poker: GSN Raises the Stakes for Poker on Television

Gavin Smith
WPT Player of the Year

The Bicycle Casino
The Gem of the West Coast

There is More to Life
Than No-Limit: Part III
By Susie Isaacs

PULL OUT
POKER GUIDE
FOR WINNING
HANDS

Poker has a long colorful history in the United States. One of the players who have been on the poker scene since its days of rounders, back rooms, and hijackings is Doyle "Texas Dolly" Brunson. He was there at the first World Series of Poker championship, and he is still a formidable player.

Changing the Game

Poker players like Doyle Brunson wanted to bring poker out of the shadows and improve its reputation and the safety of those who played. In the 1970s, with the founding of the world's first major poker tournament, the WSOP, that shift began. Benny Binion, a Las Vegas casino owner and poker enthusiast, and his son Jack began the WSOP in 1970. They were inspired by a man named Tom Moore who held a poker tournament in Reno, Nevada, the previous year.

Fans of the World Series of Poker tournament have Benny Binion (standing center, in the white cowboy hat) to thank. Benny and his family helped bring poker out of the back rooms and into the glaring lights of the biggest casinos, not just in the United States but also all over the world.

The Binions liked Moore's idea and adopted it for their own World Series, which would feature the best players on earth and crown the winner World Champion. The Binions' WSOP was an invitation-only event. Benny called on the best players he knew: Johnny Moss, "Amarillo Slim" Preston, "Sailor" Roberts, Walter "Puggy" Pearson, Crandell Addington, Carl Cannon, and Doyle "Texas Dolly" Brunson. Today those seven player are all legends in poker lore.

Johnny Moss won that first tournament, and the spectacle drew plenty of onlookers. The WSOP has been held every year since, and every year it gets bigger. Today, the tournament is open to anyone who can afford the buy-in fees. It has preliminary events followed by the main event: the $10,000 No Limit Hold'em World Championship. The winners of events receive bracelets as signs of their achievement.

For many people, those coveted bracelets are the ultimate sign of success in the high-stakes poker world. Every spring, thousands of poker greats and unknown hopefuls descend on Las Vegas, Nevada. Their destination is the Rio Hotel and Casino—today's home of the WSOP. Their hope is to become a poker superstar, and possibly a millionaire.

The Tournament Attraction

Poker tournaments brought the game out of smoky back rooms and into the public eye. Part of the attraction of tournaments is their atmosphere and excitement, but the biggest attraction is the large purse at stake.

At tournaments, every player pays a buy-in fee, a specific amount of money that allows them to enter the game. The buy-ins become one big pool for which all the players vie. For example, if one thousand people enter a tournament with a $100 buy-in, the prize pool will contain $100,000. At big tournaments, buy-ins for most events are much more, usually in the thousands and even tens of thousands of dollars. In the biggest tournament events, that money pools to create million- and multi-million-dollar prizes.

As they lose their chips, players are steadily knocked out of the tournament until only a few remain. This final table plays until only one person is left. The money from the buy-ins is then divided up among the finalists, with the winner getting the biggest prize. In an interview with Steve Marzolf for TexasHoldemPoker.com, famous poker player Jennifer Harman described the attraction of tournaments:

> **"Tournaments vs. cash games. . . . Tournaments can change people's lives. They can win a big pay day, and their life is changed forever—tournaments are over $1 million for first place. It's a small buy-in compared to the prize pool."**

In general, the prizes in tournaments are many times larger than what a person can win in a single cash game. Of course, only one person will win the big prize, but the prize is so big that lots of people are willing to sacrifice their buy-in money for a shot at the riches.

However, it's not just the money that attracts people to poker tournaments. It's also the excitement and the challenge. As former World Champion Chris Ferguson explained in an interview with Russ Scott, tournament poker has a whole different atmosphere than cash-game play:

> **"I play almost exclusively tournaments. I play a little bit of live action, but I don't like figuring out some-one's game. I just don't like taking money from people after figuring out how they play. That's just not my style. But once they put their money down for a tour-nament, it's all over. Now, that money's gone. I'm out to win the tournament. There's something to shoot for in a tournament. More than money, I think."**

Poker Revolution

Tournaments have attracted new players from diverse backgrounds and added new challenge and respectability to the game. But tourna-ments weren't the only force behind poker's evolution. Another major influence was poker literature, beginning with Doyle Brunson's book, *Super System*, in 1979. It became known as the "Bible of Poker" and was the first book to really help people understand the complex strategy and mathematical probabilities involved in the game.

Countless poker books followed, and many of them contributed to the public's growing understanding and appreciation of the game. Then, in the late eighties, something completely new entered the scene and changed the game forever: the Internet.

Of course, the Internet at that time was nothing like it is today. Just in its infancy, there was no World Wide Web and none of the poker Web sites that are now commonplace. But there was the IRC Poker

The first World Series of Poker main event brought together seven of the biggest names in poker. Today, thousands of people compete to earn a seat at the main event. They all have two things in the back of their minds—the multi-million-dollar pot and just how good those gold bracelets would look on their wrists.

Network, a text-only chat room where the computer-savvy poker players of the world could gather for play-money games. As the Internet became more sophisticated, so did online poker.

By the year 2000, poker's transformation was nearly complete. It had tournaments in casinos featuring some of the tightest and most advanced security in the world. It had books that educated players and promoted the game. And it had the Internet, which attracted even more players and allowed them to hone their skills. One of those players was Greg Raymer. And his own transformation, from a patent attorney to a poker pro, was nearly complete as well.

A New Man in Town

From his first days playing in Chicago, Greg was a cash-game player, but he was increasingly trying his hand at tournaments. He began by

THE HISTORY OF POKER

More than a thousand years ago, according to ancient writings, the Chinese emperor Mu-tsung played "domino cards" with his wife on New Year's Eve. Egyptians in the twelfth and thirteenth centuries used a form of playing cards, and in the sixteenth century, Persians used cards in a variety of betting games. A French game named "Poque" and a German game named "Pochen" became very popular in the seventeenth and eighteenth centuries. Both games developed from the sixteenth-century Spanish game called "Primero," which involved three cards being dealt to each player. Bluffing, or betting high stakes while holding poor cards to deceive opponents, was part of the game.

French colonists imported the game to North America when they arrived in Canada and New Orleans. Then poker spread via the Mississippi River's riverboats, north from New Orleans and eventually, throughout the whole country. During the Wild West period of U.S. history, a saloon with a poker table could be found in just about every Western town. The game was extremely popular during the Civil War; soldiers of both armies passed their time with hands of cards. In the twentieth century, during the world wars, poker traveled with the American troops to the rest of the world. Today, poker has become a thriving American export, with over 100 million players across the globe.

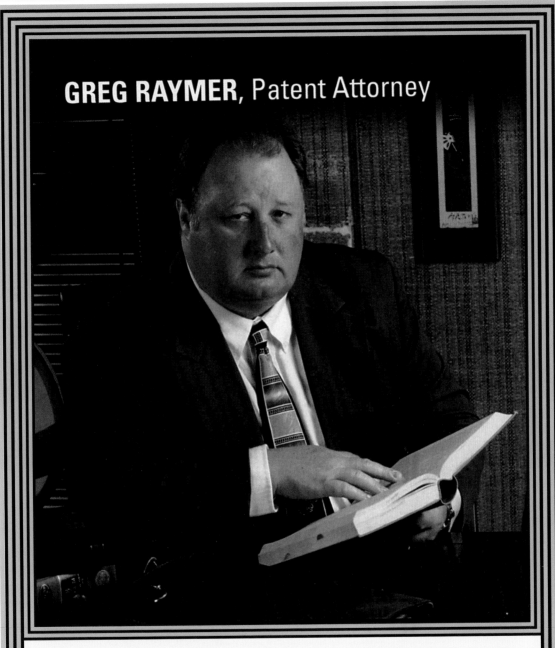

GREG RAYMER, Patent Attorney

Today's professional poker players are a diverse group. Some are well educated, others are high school dropouts. Both men and women have found success as professional players. The top names on the circuit have an international flare. And players come from all careers—including that of patent attorney, like Greg Raymer.

entering small events. The buy-ins were never more than a few hundred dollars. Often they were far less. With small buy-ins, the purse at the end was never very large, but Greg placed well in some of the tournaments and occasionally earned a few thousand dollars for his efforts.

In a few years, those purses grew. In 1998, Greg finished second in the $500 limit Hold'em event of the World Poker Finals and won $14,500. Less than six months later, he earned another $11,659 with a

Online poker games are smokin' hot. Players of all different experience levels look to online poker for additional chances to play. Some sites offer games using real money, others only allow "play" money. Even professionals like Greg (front, right) play online poker. He uses the games to help keep his skills sharp.

third-place finish in an event at the New England Poker Classic. By the end of 2000, Greg was feeling ready for bigger things. He entered the World Poker Finals again, this time finishing third in the main event. His prize was $48,960, the biggest poker payday of his career thus far. Even better, the high finish got Greg's name out on the professional poker circuit.

Greg had now proved to himself and everyone else that he was a good poker player. But that wasn't enough. He wanted to be a *great* poker player, and his recent tournament success convinced him it was possible. He knew, however, that he still had a lot of work to do if he really wanted to sit down with the best players in the world. Like a runner preparing for a marathon, he went into training. But Greg Raymer's marathon wasn't going to happen on the streets of Boston or New York. It was going to take place at the poker tables in Las Vegas in the WSOP. For this, he trained by spending hours in front of the computer screen, sharpening his skills online.

Greg had come a long way from his college days of nickel-and-dime poker games. In 2001, he took what he learned playing online and got his name on the money list at the WSOP for the first time. He finished twelfth in the $1500 Omaha Hi-Lo Split Eight or Better event. It was a milestone in his career, and it came just as the game of poker reached a milestone of its own.

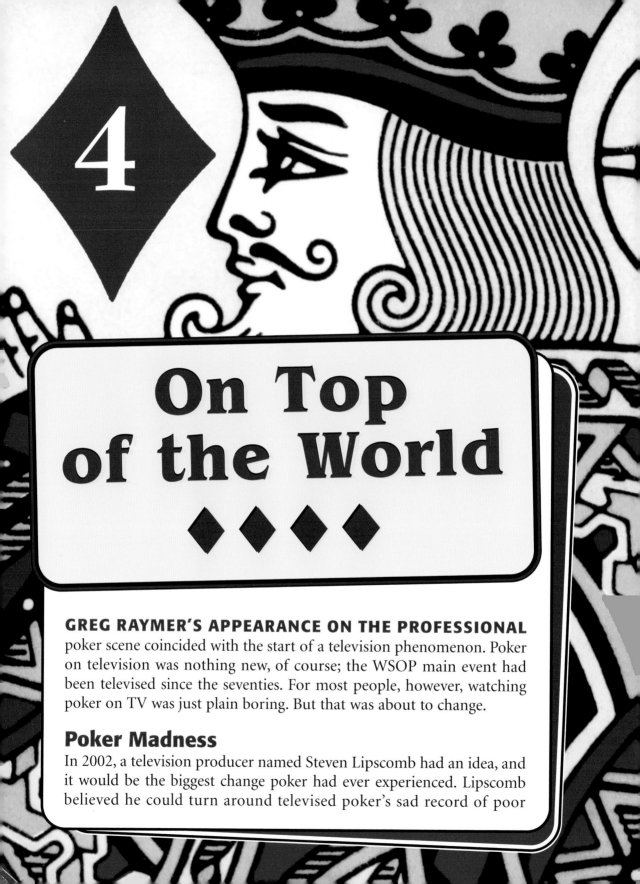

On Top of the World

◆ ◆ ◆ ◆

GREG RAYMER'S APPEARANCE ON THE PROFESSIONAL poker scene coincided with the start of a television phenomenon. Poker on television was nothing new, of course; the WSOP main event had been televised since the seventies. For most people, however, watching poker on TV was just plain boring. But that was about to change.

Poker Madness

In 2002, a television producer named Steven Lipscomb had an idea, and it would be the biggest change poker had ever experienced. Lipscomb believed he could turn around televised poker's sad record of poor

P⬥kerStars.com

Play smart!
Greg Raymer
"FossilMan"

Greg Raymer

P⬥ker Stars.c

During the early years of the twenty-first century, poker was enjoying a major growth spurt. Greg Raymer was in the right place at the right time. As the game's fan base grew, so did the number of people who learned about the Fossilman and enjoyed watching him play. Soon he was a fan favorite.

ratings. To do it, he was going to start a series of fully televised poker tournaments. He would name the project the World Poker Tour (WPT), and he believed one day it would rival the WSOP.

Many people were skeptical of Lipscomb's idea. In an interview with Larry Bills, Lipscomb remembered:

> **"I may have been the only person in the world who perceived that poker could be the next major sport. Most people thought I was crazy."**

The key to Lipscomb's success would be technology. The tour would feature the newest technological innovation for poker—a finger-sized camera mounted on the table in front of each player. This little camera would allow television viewers to see the cards (called "hole" cards or "pocket" cards) that the players held in their hands. In his interview with Russ Scott, World Champion Chris Ferguson explained why the little camera was the key to the WPT's success:

> **"The innovation that created the poker explosion in my opinion, and I think in the opinion of all the top players, is the hole-card camera. The fact that you're watching incredible professionals make incredibly intelligent decisions in real time—and you know that outcome of these decisions, you know what they should choose—makes it incredibly fun."**

Perhaps even Lipscomb could not have predicted how successful his WPT would become. The first WPT tournaments were played in 2002, and they aired on the Travel Channel in 2003. The events quickly rose to have the highest ratings of any show in Travel Channel history. Millions of people began watching the sport on TV, and a throng of poker programming hit the airwaves as other networks rushed to be part of television's next big thing.

A Media Spectacle

Television shows completed poker's transformation from a shadowy game to a popular craze. Many networks and producers are riding

All it seemed to take was a tiny little gadget called the hole cam for the game of poker to find its worldwide audience. Now, the game that was once as boring as watching grass grow was exciting to those watching from home. They had an insider's view of the game, sneaking a peak at each player's hole cards.

the wave. Today the Travel Channel broadcasts the WPT and the Professional Poker Tour. WSOP events and a program called *Pro-Am Poker Equalizer* are featured on ESPN. Bravo hosts *Celebrity Poker Showdown*, Fox Sports Net hosts the *Poker Superstars Invitational Tournament* and *Poker Dome Challenge*, NBC airs the *National Heads-Up Poker Championship* and *Poker After Dark*, and GSN has *Poker Royale* and *High Stakes Poker*.

Hollywood also likes the drama of a high-stakes poker game, and a number of movies have been made featuring real and fictional professional poker players. Some of the movies include *Rounders* with Matt Damon and Ed Norton, *Luckytown* with Kirsten Dunst, *High Roller: The Stu Ungar Story* with Michael Imperioli, and most recently, *Lucky You* with Eric Bana, Drew Barrymore, and Robert Duvall.

In addition to playing in televised tournaments, many professional poker players also appear as commentators and experts for popular poker shows. Before poker conquered America's television screens, most people had never heard the pros' names or seen their faces. The only people who had heard of people like Doyle Brunson, Jennifer Harman, and Chris Ferguson were those who played with them at the

Poker's popularity has not been limited to the small screen. Movies such as *Lucky You* have brought the game to theatergoers. The producers and directors wanted to make sure they got things right, so they brought in players as consultants, and some, like Daniel Negreanu (seated, second from left), even have small onscreen roles.

poker table. But now professional poker players are celebrities. Within a year of the WPT's first broadcasts, Greg Raymer would become a poker celebrity as well.

Raymer Arrives

Greg had some more high finishes in the 2002 World Poker Finals and the 2003 New England Poker Classic, but it was still nothing compared to what a big WSOP win would be. He continued training online, playing mostly at PokerStars.com. Then, in 2004, he entered the $160 satellite event that would lead to his world championship win.

Greg's big win in the 2004 WSOP main event was actually the second year in a row that a player had qualified at a PokerStars.com online satellite event, and then went on to win the whole thing at the WSOP. Chris Moneymaker had become famous for doing precisely the same thing the previous year. Chris Moneymaker and Greg Raymer's success encouraged others, and people turned to online play in droves, hoping that they too could one day win the big one.

Winning the World Series changed Greg's life completely. The money he won allowed him to do something he loved: play poker and be an ambassador for the game. As Greg explained in an interview for PartTimePoker.com, being a lawyer had never been his passion:

> **"I love to play poker, and I like to travel and give interviews. It is a very exciting life and you meet a lot of interesting new people. Compared to my days working as a lawyer, most of my days are stimulating and fun. My job as a lawyer wasn't particularly interesting and I didn't care about the result. The main reason I did it was to make money. There are very few jobs out there that people truly enjoy. For me poker is one of those jobs, so I feel very fortunate."**

Proving Himself

Greg's good fortune had just begun. Many people are quick to write off a person's first WSOP win as beginner's luck. But in 2005, Greg

POKER PRO

JULY 2006

WHO'S NEXT

HUCK SEED
The Art of the Bluff

WSOP HISTORY
How It All Got Started

ANNIE DUKE
Answers Your Questions

?

ONLINE TELLS

3 Champs Tell How to Win the Big One

BRACELET STRATEGY
Big-Field Tactics for Pot-Limit Omaha, Stud & Limit Hold'em

You don't have to be a household name to win a World Series of Poker championship. *Poker Pro* noted that fact in its July 2006 issue. Featured on the cover were previously unknown bracelet winners (from left) Chris Moneymaker (2003), Greg Raymer (2004), and Joe Hachem (2005). The answer to the question posed on the cover is Jamie Gold.

proved his WSOP win was no **fluke**. The field for the 2005 WSOP main event was more than double what it had been the previous year: 5,619 contestants compared to the previous year's 2,576.

Since poker's explosion on television, entries at tournaments like the WSOP have exploded as well. In the earlier days, some poker players succeeded in winning the World Championship multiple times: Doyle Brunson and Johnny Chan won the event twice, and Johnny Moss and Stu Ungar won it three times. But in these new fields of thousands of players, it's extremely unlikely that a world champion will ever again claim the prize twice. It's just too big of a field with too much luck involved. Most world champions, in fact, never even get close to the money again. But Greg Raymer did. In the 2005 WSOP main event, nine previous world champions, including Doyle Brunson, Johnny Chan, Chris Ferguson, Phil Hellmuth Jr., and Scotty Nguyen, fell on the first day of play. World champions Dan Harrington, Chris Moneymaker, and Huck Seed fell on the second day. Another fell on the fourth day.

WHO IS CHRIS MONEYMAKER?

He's one of the big names in poker—but that wasn't always the case. In 2003, Chris showed up at the World Series as a nobody in the poker world, just an accountant from Tennessee. He had won his entry into the tournament by playing a $40 satellite at PokerStars.com. After he won his trip to the WSOP, he didn't have much money for the cost of flying and staying in Vegas for the week, so he sold part of his entry to his father and a friend to cover the cost for the trip in exchange for a portion of his winnings. Chris ended up winning the World Series. He donated $25,000 of his winnings to cancer research.

Some people think Chris won because he got lucky. Others, however, acknowledge that it takes far more than luck to get where Chris is today. After his WSOP win, he went on to finish second in the WPT's Shooting Stars event, earning $200,000.

Chris's daughter Ashley was born the same year as his first big win, and now, he plans to use his winnings to put his daughter through college. In 2005, his autobiography was published, *Moneymaker: How an Amateur Poker Player Turned $40 into $2.5 Million at the World Series of Poker.*

Of all the world champions playing in the event that year, Greg Raymer lasted the longest, making it to the sixth day of play, coming in twenty-fifth overall, and claiming $304,680 in prize money. It was a major achievement that silenced any lingering doubters insistent on claiming Greg was a one-shot deal.

In addition to his huge showing in the main event, Greg also made the final table of the $1500 No Limit Hold'em event, finishing sixth and claiming $119,450 in prize money. Greg's other accomplishments for 2005 included finishing third in the first-ever British Poker Open and claiming 33rd in the $25,000 Main Event of the WPT's Third Annual Five-Star World Poker Classic. He also participated in his first major television tournament by playing in GSN's *Poker Royale: Battle of the Sexes.*

In 2006, Greg appeared in the third season of Fox Sports Net's *Poker Superstars Invitational Tournament.* That year, he also placed second in a PokerStars.com $1,000,000 tournament that had more than 1,500 players. At the WSOP, he had another great run, this time in the $5000 No Limit Deuce to Seven Draw Lowball event, where he placed fifth and earned $93,124.

His Advice to Others

In recent years, the Fossilman has proved beyond a doubt that he is a great poker player. And unlike many players of the past, he is lucky enough to be playing in an age where poker players can earn not only large sums of money but great respect as well. In his interview for PartTimePoker.com, Greg recalled how different things were when he first started out:

"When I started out playing poker thirteen years ago it wasn't something that you told your colleagues at work about. There was a big risk that they would look at you as a degenerated gambler. And it was definitely not something you put in your resume as a hobby when you applied for a job. But today people seem to have a great respect for poker players, which makes it much easier to be open about it. Most people find it exciting and want to learn how

In the 2005 World Series of Poker championship, Greg found himself up against some of the biggest names in the game, including former champs Doyle Brunson, Chris Ferguson, Johnny Chan, and others. Greg stayed at the tables longer than all the other former champs, finishing twenty-fifth. His finish helped silence critics who thought he was a one-hit wonder.

to play. From being someone that was looked upon with suspicion, the guy that plays poker has become the most popular guy at work."

When Greg gives advice to **novice** poker players, he never recommends that they jump right into the game and start taking big risks. In an interview with Russ Scott for LuckyDogPoker.com,

Practice, practice, and then practice some more. That is only some of the advice Greg gives to those just getting into the game. And they should study the game—and its players. Greg also encourages new players to resist the temptation to play with real money. Instead, he directs them to online sites where betting is done with play money.

he explained his belief that people who are new to the game should practice as they would for a sport and study as they would for school. And most important, they shouldn't risk real money. Instead, if they want to learn, he believes they should go online and play with fake money until they know what they are doing:

> **❝Play play-money games until you understand the rules, then play the penny games. Until you can win money in the penny games, don't permit yourself to play any higher. That way if you actually have or gain the ability to actually beat the game at the low levels, you're only gonna play the next step up and the next step up all the way to the top if you win the money. So, you're always playing with someone else's money, so to speak. And if you never learn to beat the games, you're down there in the penny games where a really big losing session is $5, which pretty much everyone can afford without hurting their lifestyle.❞**

Today, lots of people watch poker on television and see thousands of dollars changing hands. Sometimes it looks easy, and people get the idea that poker is a great get-rich-quick scheme. But it's an illusion. Playing winning poker takes a huge amount of skill and a good dose of luck. Even among people who have played the game for years, there are far more **net** losers than there are net winners. Only a handful of people have been able to truly win big at this game, and Greg Raymer is lucky enough to be one of them.

Just a Regular Guy

♠ ♠ ♠ ♠

GREG RAYMER IS NOW A CELEBRITY AND A MILLIONAIRE, but in many ways, his life is still the same. He is still humble and likes to play golf. His daughter and wife continue to be the most important things in his life. By most accounts, the nicest thing about Greg Raymer is that he is just a regular guy.

His New Life

In an interview for FlopTurnRiver.com, Greg explained that, although he loves playing poker, he has no interest in the party lifestyle that surrounds many of the pros:

"I almost never hang out with poker pros . . . away from the tables. I'm married with a kid, and generally boring. I like to play golf and do not drink or party. I'm more likely to hang out with the older pros, if any, and that would generally be at the golf course.**"**

In Greg's previous life as a patent attorney, he was basically anonymous. Now, as Greg Raymer poker champ, Greg gets the star treatment, thanks in large part to the media exposure the game now gets. Greg and other players are recognized when out in public, and they have their own fans.

Greg probably wouldn't have time for the celebrity lifestyle anyway. In addition to playing poker, he is a spokesperson for PokerStars.com and a public speaker. He has always been comfortable in front of a crowd—in university and law school he worked as a radio DJ, a party DJ, and a stand-up comedian—so he thoroughly enjoys his speaking engagements at conferences and corporate events.

Though Greg isn't much of a partier, that doesn't mean he's a hermit. Quite the contrary. Greg enjoys speaking to groups about poker, and he's a natural. After all, he's had a lot of experience speaking and performing in front of large crowds. He's been a DJ, a stand-up comic, and of course, an attorney.

Poker and the Game of Life

Attendees at one of Greg's events many hear him speak of the lessons people can learn from poker. As he explains on his Web site, he believes that the type of thinking that makes a great poker player can be useful to people in all different fields:

> **" In poker, there are only 52 cards, so you can estimate the opponent's cards, and quickly do some math to figure out the best decision. . . . If you make the best decision and then the cards are dealt out and you lose, you have to learn that this is irrelevant to the decision you made. It was beyond your control, and you did all that you could do that was within your power. This type of thought process is a good thing for lawyers, and for everybody. Judge somebody based upon their decisions to the greatest extent possible, rather than their results. Sometimes this is impossible, but it is what we should all strive for when evaluating somebody else's abilities in any field."**

One of the other life lessons people can learn from poker is how to control their own reactions. The person who simply reacts to life, with his anger or joy, frustration or triumph written all over his face, will not be a good poker player. He'll never be able to bluff because his opponents will see the reflection of his cards on his face! Experts say that the first step to controlling emotional reactions is to be aware of them. To be a good poker player, a person needs to become self-aware. The next step, then, is to master his emotions, so that he controls them rather than allowing them to control him. A successful poker play learns this lesson.

Poker players also need to be aware of their own limitations. They should be able to assess the situation accurately and quickly—and their own skills and weaknesses will always be a part of that equation. According to Larry W. Phillips, author of *Zen and the Art of Poker*,

> **" Years of experience eventually teach you that your main battle, always, is with yourself—your propensity**

for error, for . . . lack of concentration, misreading other players, emotional eruptions, impatience, and so on. Your opponents are merely dim outlines that come and go. Few of them can ever reach the exalted heights of damage that you can inflict on yourself."

Self-understanding and self-control are valuable life skills that help individuals handle situations far beyond a poker table. Obviously, however, other factors are involved in the poker equation, and to be successful at poker—or at life—a person needs to increase her understanding of others as well.

Learning to Read Others

Understanding others' reactions is a vital skill in nearly all aspects of human life, including intimate relationships, business, family life—and yes, poker. Ray Zee, author of *High-Low-Split Poker*, has this to say about "poker psychology":

"What I mean by the psychology of poker is getting into your opponents' heads, analyzing how they think, figuring out what they think you think, and even determining what they think you think they think."

The more aware a person is of how others around him is responding, the more control he will have of the situation. He can adjust his behaviors accordingly; he can assess the situation more accurately. Poker, experts claim, helps develop these skills.

Real life involves plenty of situations where people have to assess risk and try to interpret the best action to take next. Like poker, life requires that human beings think fast on their feet, while paying attention to both their internal states of mind, the reactions of others around them, and the simple facts of the situation. Some may call this using intelligence. Others disagree and think people don't have to be "smart" to have these skills; instead, they need to have **intuition**—or else just plain luck.

In the end, whether poker players depend on skill, intuition, or simply luck, they must be able to handle both the excitement of

What does it take to become a great poker player? One of the most important skills for a poker player to have is the ability to read other players. One of the best at getting into the minds of opponents is Jennifer Harman, the winner of two World Series of Poker bracelets.

winning and, more often than not, the disappointment of losing. Learning to not become overconfident after a win is an important skill, and so is being able to bounce back after a loss. Whether it's the game of Texas Hold'em—or the game of life—the challenge to improve one's game never ends. It's a challenge the Greg Raymer has taken on, and it's one that he intends to win.

Greg is still evolving as a poker player, developing the skills necessary to read his opponents and anticipate their moves. He's proved that he's good at it, and everyone thinks that he'll only get better the more he plays. Greg thinks so too, and he plans to add more bracelets to his wrist and trophies to his trophy case.

The Next Vice President?

Greg is now a world champion, a public speaker, and a celebrity, but could he be the next vice president of the United States? In his interview for HoldEmBack.com, Greg talked about the possibility of running for vice president as a candidate for the Libertarian Party in 2008. He stated that the recent passage of new anti-gambling

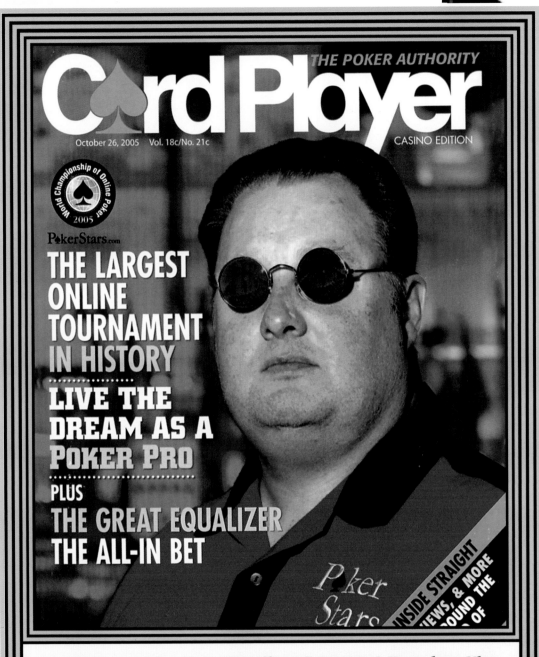

THE POKER AUTHORITY

C♠rd Player

CASINO EDITION

October 26, 2005   Vol. 18c/No. 21c

PokerStars.com

THE LARGEST ONLINE TOURNAMENT IN HISTORY

LIVE THE DREAM AS A POKER PRO

PLUS

THE GREAT EQUALIZER THE ALL-IN BET

So what's next for Greg "Fossilman" Raymer? How does Vice President Raymer sound? Well, it's not as far-fetched as it might sound at first. He's mentioned that he might seek the Libertarian Party nomination for the vice presidency in 2008. Among the issues he'd like to tackle is recent anti-gambling legislation.

TEENS AND POKER

According to a 2007 study, 2.9 million teenagers play some form of poker. Poker paraphernalia intended for kids is for sale everywhere, from supermarkets to stores like Spencers and even Toys R Us. Not everyone is happy about this; gambling addiction experts warn that poker could be a slippery slope into other high-risk activities—but others disagree.

Barry Shulman, publisher of *Card Player* magazine, told *USA Today* that poker offers teens five beneficial things:

- social interaction, especially for the socially awkward
- help with math and other numbers-related skills
- an understanding of risk/reward **scenarios**
- lessons on how to read looks and gestures
- insights into personal limits and self-control

Not everyone, however, agrees that poker is a positive activity, and particularly not for young people. Research indicates individuals who begin gambling before the age of eighteen are far more likely to develop gambling addictions as adults. (An addiction means that gamblers continue to gamble despite negative consequences; they may even *want* to quit, but they can't.)

Some gambling experts warn that poker could also introduce young adults to other risky activities, such as drug abuse. "Kids are gambling with their health [when they play poker], because for some people this can get very serious indeed," said Keith Whyte, executive director of the nonprofit National Council on Problem Gambling. The council's studies show that among kids who gamble, 50 percent binge drink, and 75 percent smoke marijuana.

ABC recently reported the story of a young adult who ran into problems with poker. He started out enjoying neighborhood card games, but during a summer in Mexico, he progressed to betting larger and larger amounts. Eventually, he was $20,000 in debt. What happened next scared him:

"I can't pinpoint it exactly, but I had a strong sense that I was out of control. My reaction to getting out of the hole was to bet more—it wasn't to stop and find help."

legislation as well as disagreements with the philosophies of the current administration has made him consider the move to politics:

> **"I never seriously considered politics in the past, but all of the mess we are having in the poker world lately, most of which can be traced to a silly administration, has me thinking about it more and more. . . . I understand that it is highly unlikely that anybody running for President or VP on the Libertarian ticket will be elected to that office, but I am hopeful that I can help the Libertarian Party get more attention and more votes, and that this will lead us to becoming a major party a few elections down the road."**

Greg went on to describe his belief in **tolerance** and liberty, and why he thinks people should have an open-minded approach, not just to poker but to life:

> **"A lot of people cannot seem to grasp the difference between morals and intolerance. They believe that if they see something as bad, that it must be bad, and they have a duty to stop us from participating. However, what they fail to see is that I might see something as bad that they consider good, and that if I acted like them when I was in power, they would lose what they see as a right. In other words, they are incapable of putting on the other shoe, and seeing the world from somebody else's point of view. And that is intolerance."**

Tolerance, respect, and personal liberty are very important to Greg. Without them, he and other professional poker players could never achieve what they have today, and Greg is willing to work hard to protect these things. But even if he decides against the move to politics, he will continue to be in the public eye for years to come as Fossilman, one of the best poker players in the world.

CHRONOLOGY

1820s   Modern versions of poker first appear in the United States.

1964   **June 25** Greg Raymer is born in Minot, North Dakota.

1970   The first World Series of Poker (WSOP) is played at Binion's Horseshoe casino.

1979   Doyle Brunson's *Super System* is published.

1992   Greg graduates from law school and begins his law career.

1995   Greg makes a deal with his wife to set aside $1,000 for poker; if he loses the money, he will quit playing forever.

1996   Greg begins selling fossils, earning the nickname Fossilman.

1998   Greg finishes second in a World Poker Finals event.

1999   Greg and his family relocate to Connecticut, and he begins playing at Foxwoods Resort and Casino; he finishes third in a New England Poker Classic event.

2000   Greg places third in the World Poker Finals main event and gets first real recognition on the professional circuit; has his first high WSOP finish.

2002   The hole cam comes to the United States; the World Poker Tour (WPT) begins.

2003   The first television broadcasts of the WPT air and become the highest-rated show in Travel Channel history.

2004   Greg wins an online satellite tournament and goes on to become World Champion at the WSOP.

2005   Greg finishes twenty-fifth in the WSOP main event.

2006   Greg places second in a PokerStars.com $1,000,000 tournament and fifth in a WSOP event.

Accomplishments & Awards

World Series of Poker Wins
2004 $10,000 No Limit Holdem Main Event

Selected Television Appearances
2005   *Poker Royale: Battle of the Sexes*

2006   *Poker Superstars Invitational Tournament*

Further Reading & Internet Resources

Books

Ackerman, Loren, and Christopher Ackerman. *Talkin' About Poker: Straight Talk for Parents and Their Players.* Hackettstown, N.J.: High Powered Publishing LLC, 2006.

Fornatale, Peter. *Winning Secrets of Poker.* New York: DRF Press, 2006.

Kaplan, Michael, and Brad Reagan. *Aces and Kings: Inside Stories and Million Dollar Strategies from Poker's Greatest Players.* New York: Wenner Books, 2006.

Nosek, Jude. *Poker Night Handbook: A Guide for Getting a Game Together and Keeping It Fun and Exciting.* Oak Park, Ill.: KnackPacks, 2002.

Web Sites

www.allinmag.com
All In

www.bluffmagazine.com
Bluff

www.cardplayer.com
Card Player

www.fossilman.com
Greg Raymer's Official Web Site

www.gamblersanonymous.org
Gambler's Anonymous Official Homepage

www.pokerpages.com
Poker Pages

www.thehendonmob.com
The Hendon Mob

www.worldpokertour.com
World Poker Tour

GLOSSARY

amateur—Someone who participates in an activity for pleasure rather than for pay.

circuit—A series of ongoing competitions.

fluke—Something surprising or unexpected that happens by accident.

holographic—Used to describe a three-dimensional image created by using a photographic plate and light from a laser.

intuition—The state of being aware of or knowing something without having to discover it through intelligence or perceive it with the senses.

motley—Consisting of people or things that are very different from one another.

net—The amount left after accounting for all necessary deductions.

novice—Someone who lacks experience.

patent—An exclusive right granted by the government to an inventor to make or sell inventions for a specified period of time.

satellite—A tournament that is associated with a larger, more prestigious one.

scenarios—Imagined sequences of possible events.

tolerance—The acceptance of differing views of other people.

SELECT POKER TERMS

All-in—When you have put all of your playable money and chips into the pot during the course of a hand.

Ante—A prescribed amount posted before the start of a hand by all players.

Bet—The act of placing a wager in turn into the pot on any betting round, or the chips put into the pot.

Big blind—The largest regular blind in a game.

Blind—A required bet made before any cards are dealt.

Bluff—A bet or raise with a hand that is unlikely to beat the other players.

Board card—A community card in the center of the table, as in Hold'em or Omaha.

Button—A player who is in the designated dealer position.

Buy-in—The minimum amount of money required to enter any game.

Check—To waive the right to initiate the betting in a round.

Check-raise—To waive the right to bet until a bet has been made by an opponent, and then to increase the bet by at least an equal amount when it is your turn to act.

Community cards—The cards dealt face up in the center of the table that can be used by all players to form their best hand in the games of Hold'em and Omaha.

Cut—To divide the deck into two sections in such a manner as to change the order of the cards.

Discards(s)—In a draw game, the card(s) thrown away; the muck.

Face card—A king, queen, or jack.

Fixed limit—In limit poker, any betting structure in which the amount of the bet on each particular round is pre-set.

Flop—In Hold'em or Omaha, the three community cards that are turned simultaneously after the first round of betting.

Fold—To throw a hand away and relinquish all interest in a pot.

Heads-up play—Only two players involved in play.

Kicker—The highest unpaired card that helps determine the value of a five-card poker hand.

Loose—Playing more hands than normal.

Muck—(1) The pile of discards gathered facedown in the center of the table by the dealer; (2) To discard a hand.

Over card—A hole card that is higher than any other card on the board.

Play the board—Using all five community cards for your hand in Hold'em.

Pot-limit—The betting structure of a game in which you are allowed to bet up to the amount of the pot.

Raise—To increase the amount of a previous wager.

River—The final card dealt.

Showdown—The final act of determining the winner of the pot after all betting has been completed.

Small blind—In a game with multiple blind bets, the smallest blind.

Split pot—A pot that is divided among players, either because of a tie for the best hand or by agreement prior to the showdown.

Suited—Cards are of the same suit.

Tight—Playing fewer hands than normal.

Tight game—A game with less players than normal in fewer hands.

Turn—The fourth card dealt on the board during community card games.

SELECT POKER SLANG

All blue—A flush containing either clubs or spades.

All pink—A flush containing either diamonds or hearts.

Back door—Making a hand that the player wasn't drawing at.

Bad beat—A hand being beat by another hand that had a very low percentage of becoming a winning hand.

Cards speak—The face value of a hand in a showdown is the true value of the hand, regardless of a verbal announcement.

Drawing dead—Drawing to a hand that cannot win because someone already holds a hand that will beat what you are drawing to.

Potting out—Agreeing with another player to take money out of a pot, often to buy food, cigarettes, or drinks, or to make side bets.

Rags—Cards generally not worth playing.

Dolly Parton—A hand containing a 9 and a 5.

Rocket cards—Two aces.

Jackson 5—Jack and a five.

Pocket rockets—Two aces dealt face down.

Big slick—Ace and a king.

Ducks—Two 2s.

Paint—Any face card.

Rainbow—Three or four cards of different suits.

Nuts—The best possible hand.

TEXAS HOLD'EM HAND RANKINGS

The top ten Texas Hold'em hands in descending order of rank and the odds of seeing one when playing Texas Hold'em poker.

(1) ROYAL FLUSH

A | K | Q | J | 10
♠ | ♠ | ♠ | ♠ | ♠

A Ten-to-Ace straight, all in one suit
Odds against getting one: 30,939-to-1

(2) STRAIGHT FLUSH

Q | J | 10 | 9 | 8
♦ | ♦ | ♦ | ♦ | ♦

A run of five card values, all in one suit
Odds against getting one: 3,590-to-1

(3) FOUR OF A KIND

7 | 7 | 7 | 7 | K
♦ | ♣ | ♥ | ♠ | ♥

All four cards of the same value
Odds against getting one: 594-to-1

(4) FULL HOUSE

9 | 9 | 9 | J | J
♦ | ♣ | ♠ | ♦ | ♥

Three of a kind, plus a pair (any suits)
Odds against getting one: 37.5-to-1

(5) FLUSH

K | J | 8 | 5 | 3
♥ | ♥ | ♥ | ♥ | ♥

Five cards (any values) in the same suit
Odds against getting one: 32.1-to-1

(6) STRAIGHT

A | 2 | 3 | 4 | 5
♣ | ♦ | ♥ | ♣ | ♠

A run of five card values, in any suits
Odds against getting one: 20.6-to-1

(7) THREE OF A KIND

4 | 4 | 4 | 6 | Q
♣ | ♥ | ♠ | ♠ | ♥

Three cards of the same value
Odds against getting one: 19.7-to-1

(8) TWO PAIR

10 | 10 | K | K | 2
♣ | ♦ | ♠ | ♦ | ♣

Two sets of two cards of the same value
Odds against getting one: 3.26-to-1

(9) ONE PAIR

5 | 5 | 6 | A | 9
♣ | ♦ | ♥ | ♠ | ♣

Two cards of the same value
Odds against getting one: 1.28-to-1

(10) HIGH CARD ONLY

A | 10 | 9 | 5 | 3
♥ | ♣ | ♦ | ♠ | ♥

A hand with no pairs, straight, or flush
Odds against getting one: 4.74-to-1

INDEX

About the Author

Mitch Roycroft is a professional children's writer who has written numerous books and articles for young people. Mitch has lived in the United States, Canada, and Africa, currently resides in Toronto, Ontario, and is contemplating a move to Europe. Mitch enjoys playing poker with friends, but he doesn't like to play for money.

Picture Credits

page

9: WSOP/FPSP
11: AdverMedia Archive
12: MaxSports Archive
15: MaxSports Archive
17: Starstock/Photoshot
18: MaxSports Archive
21: WSOP/FPSP
23: New Millennium Images
24: ReflectFoto Collection
27: WSOP/FPSP
29: PokerStars.com/NMI
30: MaxSports Archive

33: PokerStars.com/NMI
35: WPT/PRNPS
36: Warner Bro. Pictures/NMI
38: New Millennium Images
41: WSOP/FPSP
42: Starstock/Photoshot
45: Starstock/Photoshot
46: PPA/UBM
49: Full Tilt/AdverMedia Archive
50: MaxSports Archive
51: New Millennium Images

Front cover: AdverMedia Archive